Letter to *my* Father

Bernard Marin

**HARVARD
PUBLICATIONS**

First published in 2020
by Harvard Publications
432 St Kilda Road
Melbourne 3004

This book is copyright. Apart from any fair dealing for the purpose of private study, research, criticism or review as permitted by the *Copyright Act 1968*, no part may be reproduced by any process without written permission from the publisher.

Copyright © Bernard Marin 2020

The moral right of the author has been asserted.

A catalogue record for this book is available from the National Library of Australia

ISBN 978 0 6485553 3 9

Design by Skeleton Gamblers Creative

Letter to *my* Father

Bernard Marin

In memory of my father
Stanislaw Marin

Dear Dad

In the year I turned forty-eight I began to suffer from severe headaches. At the same age, you had suffered a heart attack and a stroke, and your father had died in Europe at the age of forty-eight.

My family doctor diagnosed migraines and referred me to a psychiatrist, who soon determined that I had never grieved for you. I was shocked. But then how do you mourn the loss of somebody you never really knew?

Today, twenty years later and thirty-three years after your death, I am sitting at my desk looking out the window and reflecting on our troubled relationship. Franz Kafka's *Letter to Father* lies open before me, and I am suddenly prompted to write to you.

As hailstones strike the window and lightning flashes, I am reminded for some reason of the cigarette lighter I gave you as a present when I was sixteen or so. The metal lighter was enclosed in a fine network of filaments, like vines twisting around a tree. I had saved for months to buy it, all the money I'd earned from washing cars and doing other odd jobs.

'It's beautiful,' you said.

'I figured it's something you could really use,' I replied, gratified to have pleased you.

I looked forward to seeing you flicking off the lid to light up your endless Craven A cigarettes, feeling that I now had some small part in your life.

A few days later I was talking to my brother Paul when he took out a cigarette and held out the lighter to light one for me, too. I sat there, quite still, looking at the lighter. I could feel myself turning pale.

'Where did you get that lighter?' I asked.

'Oh, I lost my other lighter, so Dad gave me this one,' Paul said. 'I guess he didn't want it.'

'He's a bastard,' I said.

Paul shrugged and lit his cigarette. 'Don't get so worked up,' he said, blowing out a mouthful of smoke. 'You'll give yourself a seizure.'

Thinking about that lighter now, more than fifty years later, I feel the same stab of pain and anger towards you, with your callous silence, your emotional incapacity. It was just one of the thousand tiny betrayals I felt throughout my childhood. But most of all I am angry that, like a cricketer who wasn't needed, I was left on the bench for so long, unwanted and forgotten.

Back then, I certainly didn't understand you or your behaviour. I wondered what it was that made you close yourself off from the world, from me, and shut out everything with a determination you never showed in any other part of your life.

Compare the two of us: same oval face, hazel eyes, straight nose and regular mouth, protruding ears. As I've grown older I've developed your round shoulders and barrel chest. You had a good head for figures, and so do I.

Your talent aided your great appetite for gambling. When I was doing research for *My Father, My Father*, the book I published in 2002, I went to see your estranged business partner. Sol told me, 'I saw your dad in a café in Acland Street tossing a coin with some guy. The fella said, "What's the stake? Hundred quid?" Stan said, "Make it five hundred." It was stupid. I knew he didn't have money like that. I could see his eyes glittering. They chucked up the coin. Stan called heads. He won the first toss. Then the guy said, "Double or nothing?" and Stan said, "Sure." A second toss, and it was heads again, and now your dad was up £1000. They bet again – and Stan won. They kept doubling the ante, and doubling again, until Stan was richer by £32,000. It was a goddamn fortune. But Stan wouldn't stop. He called heads again. The coin went up and came down tails. They shook hands and walked away. He lost £32,000. I would have gone in and talked to him. But then I got a look at his face, and for once he looked happy. It didn't matter whether he won or lost, your father loved to gamble. His father was a gambler, and gambling connected him to his father.'

I remember your poker nights. You used to play every Friday night, at different houses. Every few weeks you'd have it at our place. I recall lying in bed, hearing the shouts of excitement from the den, muffled by the glass doors. It must have gone all night. Next day, the house would be full of stale tobacco fumes. Paul and

I used to go into the kitchen and pinch the cakes and savouries that Mum made. Sometimes I watched you playing cards. You looked happy. I remember thinking you'd be happy to die playing cards. And in the end, you did. I never really understood your passion for gambling. You had a wife and family who loved you. But the only thing that made you happy was gambling. It was like a sickness.

Once I received a letter from your old army friend, Rudi, recalling your gambling during the war. 'In May 1945 we rehearsed the landings in Borneo and Morotai. We were stuck on the bloody ship for two weeks doing nothing, trying to sleep in shifts, sandwiched between the landing gear and the tanks. There was a lot of waiting. Les Anderson and your dad saved everyone from going bonkers in the heat and the boredom and the stale air with their gambling ventures. First, they started a two-up school down in the hull. It was pretty small stuff, but a lot of fun. Then they started an SP bookie on boat races (using what beer we had) below deck. Les and your dad separated everyone into two equal teams, stood them in two lines, side by side, with a pint of beer each. Your dad shouted, "Go!" and the first person on each team gulped their pint and placed the empty glass upside down on his head. As soon as he did this the next person started drinking, and so on. It was great fun and it kept us occupied – we all lost our army pay but didn't even mind.'

Every Saturday you loved sitting in the dining room studying the form guide, going to the TAB and returning home to listen to Burt Bryant and Ken Howard calling races on the radio. I recall you punching the air with excitement when your horse won, or banging your fist on the table and shouting, 'Fuckin' donkey!' when your horse lost.

The prospect of your violent anger always scared me. I never understood it – it would blow in from nowhere like a sudden dust cloud, and then disappear again, just as suddenly, into the calm, grey sky. It was usually associated with some act of defiance by Paul, but it always seemed to have some other element – a kind of passionate fury, which, to my mind, exceeded the circumstances. It rarely resulted in actual violence but rather in an impotent rage, from which Paul seemed to derive some strange satisfaction. I had always felt excluded from this strange symbiosis, always trying instead to please you through obedience and righteousness. This earned me Paul's vengeance, and he would vent on me the powerlessness he felt in relation to you, which often led to him being punished once again. Thus, somehow, we became the bad son and the good son, the delinquent and the angel. They were parts we played up to, and they slowly become unquestioned elements of our respective selves. Doubtless they drew on some fundamental grain of our personalities, but they grew into a dynamic whose strength I never quite understood, even as it shaped the complexion of my childhood.

Paul bore the brunt of your rages. He was forever getting into trouble. I recall you bought a couple of brand-new Malvern Star bicycles, out of the blue, which must have cost a fortune back then. One day I was in the backyard and I could hear you screaming, 'You fucking idiot, Paul!' He had decided to dismantle the bike, bit by bit, ball bearing by ball bearing, to learn about its inner workings. Paul fought with you a lot; I didn't.

I remember another incident from the early years. I was only nine or ten at the time, and Paul, who was boisterous, adventurous and fearless, had started the Daredevils Club. The older boys in the street had been picking on him, and he started the club as a way of distracting their attention or gaining their respect. Club members were compelled to do acts of idiocy. One time, Paul decided that we should steal something from Davies' paper shop. It would be a marker of our manhood.

'Nice try, sonny,' Mr Davies said when he caught Paul. 'I should really call the cops. Count yourself lucky if I only call up your parents.'

By chance Dad was not home when Mr Davies telephoned. Mum listened for quite a while and then apologised. She hung up the phone and just then the mother of one of the other club members called.

Mum put down the phone and said, 'Faye thinks I shouldn't tell your father. She's worried he'll lose his temper.'

Mum told you what had happened, but you were not angry with me, nor did you lecture me. You avoided me, and within a week the matter was forgotten. When I realised that I would not be punished for my part in the crime I felt a cool relief wash over me. But somehow, in my heart, I felt as though a door had closed against me. Every time you avoided my eyes, I felt I had been banished, sent to some faraway place, growing smaller and smaller until I was out of sight. I don't know why you behaved that way. Was it because you were disappointed in me? Was it that you thought I was too sensitive to be punished? Or did you consider I had learnt my lesson? I felt completely alone and isolated, as though you had disappeared forever, leaving me behind.

After that incident, I may have been more obedient, but I came away from it with internal damage. I suspect it crystallised my sense of abandonment and exposed the failings in our relationship. It clarified my belief that you had turned away from me, leaving me with a feeling of rejection, a fear that I still carry today. It also heightened my craving for love and affection, which continues to mark my life.

I remember one Saturday afternoon when you and Mum had gone out and I was at home alone. Somehow, I broke the glass top of the table in the lounge and was paralysed with fear waiting for you and Mum to come home. I sat indoors, peering through the window, my friends playing out in the street. I felt pitiful, scared. You didn't punish me then, either, but it never felt like love or concern; it felt more like indifference.

Because I had seen Paul being punished on numerous occasions I was terrified that I might suffer the same fate – that you might discipline me. That of course meant I lived in fear of you. Punishment suspended or delayed is far more terrifying for a child. A quick, even painful punishment that is soon over is preferable.

For a long time I suffered from the tormenting fantasy that you – my father, the ultimate authority, the person who could do no wrong, the all-knowing one I had put on a pedestal – might fly off the handle for nothing more than a boisterous prank, scream and shout and punish me, thus proving that I was a mere nothing to you. I retreated into my room and my private world of breeding tropical fish. Guppies, Siamese fighting fish and swordtails became my refuge from your potential tirades.

Back then I was shy and self-conscious, lacking confidence, a quiet, fearful child.

I was always scared you would shout at me. I longed for your attention, your approval, for a kind word, and therefore I was not terribly difficult to handle. A friendly look, a quiet taking by the hand, would have meant a great deal, but you seemed emotionally vacant. You never once told me you loved me.

But I don't want you to think it was all bad. I have many fond memories of your nursery, 'The Patch', in Ferntree Gully. It was there, on the edge of the city, where the foothills of the Dandenongs rise steeply towards densely forested peaks, that I once had a father – a warm, lively man, in a dark 1950s suit, with his shirt sleeves rolled up, standing in the middle of the potted herbs and geraniums and rhododendrons of his nursery. In the face of the child by your side I can see the same childish pride I felt every Sunday afternoon at being allowed to assist you with the business of planting and growing and watering and weeding. Sometimes I helped the local gardeners pick out the shrubs or rockery plants for their quarter-acre blocks and nature strips: pig face, agapanthus, Chinese lanterns, spider plants, zinnias, pink and violet fuchsias, crimson azaleas, white hibiscus. I was captivated by this profusion of life and colour, this certainty, this love.

I recall my thriving little vegetable garden, which I tended religiously at the back of the nursery. All weekend I pottered and basked in the sense of security and closeness that came from being together with you in the bright clear sunlight.

Sometimes you talked with friends and business acquaintances and customers. I don't remember the conversations – the low, reassuring murmur was all I needed. Meanwhile, I wandered up and down the gravelled rows with a watering can, watching the seedlings poke their first green shoots out of the moist earth. In the permanent noon of childhood, I believed the sun would always be shining, and the sprinklers always glistening, and that you, that man in the dark grey pants, your sleeves rolled up to your elbows, would be there, always murmuring or laughing around the next row of gardenias.

But you weren't. Somewhere along the way you became that stranger, that distant silent foreigner. What happened? I remember the dry, empty feeling, a feeling I have learned to accept, but now, thinking back, I am taken off guard once again by the memory of some real happiness, by the memory that there was once a time when I had a father.

Back then it never occurred to me, but I now realise you must have cared, because I remember one night when I was very small you came into my room to check that I was asleep. I was dimly aware of your presence in the room, but I did not show that I was awake. The light was falling through the partly open door behind your shoulder, sending warm yellow waves into my room. You stood there for a long time. Then I opened my eyes a tiny crack and everything was dark again. You had left the room as silently as you had entered.

To others, you could be a kind, soft-hearted person. Paul often delights in telling the story of when a man, apparently an old acquaintance of yours who you had not seen for many years, turned up at the front door requesting money, and you, without hesitation, pulled out your wallet and handed him some cash. And I recall Mum's frustration and complaints when you went out for dinner with friends and insisted on paying the bill.

You dominated my world; your opinion was right; every other was wrong. You could, for instance, rail at the capitalist system, not only selectively but in every respect. At least so it seemed to me.

There was hardly ever any conversation between us, but when there was, you were often right. Like other children, I was influenced by your thinking. Not that there was anything incomprehensible about that. After all, I had put you on a pedestal and you could do, or say, no wrong.

What was always incomprehensible to me was your utter lack of sensitivity to me; it was as if you had no notion of your power.

Thinking back, maybe I should not have expected enthusiasm from you for every childish triviality when you were burdened by financial concerns and past traumas. But that was not the point. The point was much more that your failure to acknowledge any of my achievements always disappointed me. Your whole method of child-rearing was like this. I never received any praise or encouragement from you. Unlike other fathers, you never came to my school or sporting events.

As a young boy, I idolised the god-like test players, Ritchie Benaud and Garfield Sobers. I imagined that one day I would step out onto Lord's or the MCG as a test cricketer in a glorious battle for the Ashes. You never showed up to a single game of cricket in all the years that I played for school or the Ormond Cricket Club. While the other fathers cheered from the sidelines you were always 'hard at work' or 'needing to finish something'. When we won the Under-16 Premiership I rated a mention in the club annual. I rushed home and found you in the backyard reading the newspaper and smoking. Having underlined my achievement, I gave the annual to you. You looked at it, nodded mutely and handed it back.

'You'll never be tall enough to be an opening batsman,' you said.

'Well, Bradman wasn't that tall,' I stammered.

'I don't know why you try so hard. It's a waste of time. No matter how good you are, you're never going to play for Australia.'

I can still hear your low voice as you walked away. 'They'd never pick a Jew.'

The five years after I turned sixteen in 1966 brought change, all of it for the worse. I was no longer the dynamic rover on the football field darting in and out of the packs, or the slips fieldsman and wicket keeper with lightning reflexes. I stopped playing sport altogether. My schoolwork, too, degenerated alarmingly. I became quiet, self-conscious, introverted and shy. My self-esteem faltered, and I felt estranged from my friends.

Watching my decline, you only expressed a distant regret that at times seemed like indifference and at other times like disappointment. 'You carry the weight of the world on your shoulders, Bernard,' you often remarked. But your detachment from my life, like a tourist passing through on his way somewhere else, was part of the burden that was pulling my shoulders into a stoop, curving my spine, and etching the first faint lines on my teenage brow.

Our inability to really talk to each other had yet another effect. I wouldn't have become a particularly eloquent speaker in any case, but I would at least have mastered the usual fluency of everyday language. But your remark that 'children should be seen and not heard' has been with me since very early on. I acquired in your presence a hesitant manner of speaking and eventually, because of your erratic temper and my desire for your approval, I kept silent. This need for approval has continued to affect me throughout my life.

I am the way I am as a result of my upbringing, and of course I had two parents, not one. Mum also influenced me. She was an only child who had spent her whole early life taking directions from others; that's how she was brought up. Before you came along, she did what her parents, her teachers, or her employer told her to do, and, although she had a mind of her own, she was happy to yield to you and follow your lead, even if, at times, it was against her better judgement. She kept house – cleaning, cooking and washing clothes – and when you came home from a long day, she had dinner waiting for us on the table. I knew she would always take your side. She loved and respected you and that's what women of her generation did.

Mum was a bright and capable student. She graduated from University High School, enrolled at Pharmacy College but, at the last minute, decided not to proceed. I recall walking into the kitchen one morning and seeing her standing at the sink wearing her yellow rubber gloves. She seemed deep in thought.

'What's up?' I asked.

'Oh!' She snapped upright, jerking back from the sink as she dropped a plate into the water.

'I was thinking about College.'

'What College?' I asked.

'If I have one regret in my life,' she continued, 'it's that I didn't study pharmacy.'

'Why do you say that?'

'Because I think I would be more independent if I had, less reliant on your father and, maybe, a much more fulfilled person.' She sighed.

'But you're happily married and your family and friends love you …'

She did not respond.

'You have a passion for the world and its issues and you're selfless and well-intentioned. What more could you ask for?'

'I wish Grandpa had made me do pharmacy,' she said in a small voice as she turned off the tap and placed the plate in the drying rack.

At meal times whatever was brought to the table had to be eaten up. Mum insisted we eat everything no matter the gagging and the long refusals to comply. It was wrong to waste food. 'Think yourself lucky,' you shouted. 'During the war people had nothing to eat.' Those words carried with them a darkness that I never understood. Today it is different; I understand their source.

Your volatile temper, Dad, was an extremely effective child-rearing device, which never failed with me. I cannot remember you scolding me directly or speaking with explicitly abusive language. It wasn't really necessary, you had so many other means, and in conversation at home your criticisms flew all around me; as a small boy I was overwhelmed by them and had no reason not to apply them to myself, for the people you were abusing were certainly no worse than me, and you were certainly no more dissatisfied with them than with me. And here too was your puzzling innocence about your own behaviour: you lost your temper and screamed without the slightest scruple, yet you disliked such behaviour in others.

As a child, I believed everything that you said was a commandment from heaven. I have never forgotten your words, which have stayed with me as the most important means for judging the world.

Your child-rearing methods in the very early years I cannot, of course, describe. Like most fathers in the fifties and sixties, you were often absent, completely tied to work, to earning money, hardly able to be with me at all.

This is how the world came to be divided into two parts for me: one in which I, the obedient, shy child wanting to please, lived under laws that had to be obeyed; and then a second world where my friends seemed to live happily and free from oppression.

Wendy, my wife, has always described my brother Paul and me as 'chalk and cheese'. I recall one evening when Paul came to our place for dinner. He was recently divorced and stood around in the kitchen with self-conscious ease in a tight black top and flared jeans, his long, curly black hair falling to his shoulders. He chatted casually about his practice as a barrister and the unconventional – often criminal – clients he defended. I noticed that he enjoyed playing up the sense of adventure, excitement and uncertainty of his job. He made a point of saying that the only thing holding him here in the suburbs was his commitment to his kids.

I wondered how we had ended up so different, he still so energetic and unconventional, so centred on youthfulness, while I had chosen, equally deliberately, the role of father, husband, accountant, committee member and pillar of the community.

When I look at the photographs of us as children, I'm always the one standing back slightly, diffident, retreating a little from the camera. Paul is full of restless energy, edging forward, as if he is about to burst out of the frame. And he is no different now. Creeping reluctantly towards his seventies – he is still on the same quest for novelty and excitement, with the same impatience and distracted intelligence. To me, his life is too disorganised, too chaotic. I can't see how he can stand it. Yet we manage to maintain a strong connection nonetheless – not as friends, but as brothers. Sometimes I wonder if it is the bond of two orphans.

I recall sitting in my study one evening talking to Paul when I was writing my family memoir.

'Look, Dad had his problems,' he said. 'God knows we fought enough. You're the one that got along with him.'

'That's because I was scared of him,' I said. 'I made a point of not fighting with him.'

'Yeah. You never got into trouble. You were always the good son.'

'I didn't choose that. Did you choose to be the bad one?'

'Well, it was just my character. Anyway, it wasn't all fighting.'

'Really?' I asked. 'What else do you remember about him, apart from the fighting?'

Paul stared at me. He looked as if he was about to reply, but he didn't say anything for a long time. He looked away. 'I know there were other things,' he said. 'I just can't think of them now.'

'Okay,' I said. 'Do you ever remember him coming to one of your football matches?'

'Yeah,' Paul said. 'I think he came a couple of times.'

'Well he never came to a single one of mine.'

'You know he was a workaholic, so maybe he didn't have the time. Why do you get so worked up about it?'

'Because I would have given anything for him to come to just one. But he never did.'

Paul leaned back in his chair, looking uncomfortable and irritated by the conversation. He stared at me for a moment, got up and said, 'I've got to go – someone is waiting for me.'

'How'd you get into business together?' I asked Sol as we sat in the sun in his lounge room reminiscing about my father.

'Well, a couple of years after the war, your father came to me with a proposal: we should buy out my brother Alec's coat-making business. He had done a bit of work as a cutter with his Uncle Leon in handbags and such, so he could see the opportunity. But, of course, he didn't have a copper nickel to his name. So, he needed to get terms with Alec, and that's what we did. And we made our money back in a couple of years and sold the business at a profit.'

'Dad always said that your Chapel Street operation made a lot of money.'

'Well, that really wasn't business, now was it? It was … a little venture on the far side of the law, shall we say. Anyway, we got busted, named in the papers, police at the house. We had to know when to walk away. The sandwich bar – now that was a proper business, and we made not too bad a profit on it, too. We bought another one in La Trobe Street in the city. Sold that and started a construction business. And then the nurseries. They were a financial disaster. We got back into building and hooked up with Colt & Co. Real Estate in Ripponlea for a couple of years. Then we set up on our own in Jules Meltzer's building. Rent free. Then I was offered a partnership at a real estate firm and because we had always done everything together I brought your father in.'

To me, your many businesses over the years evidenced your restlessness, your inability to settle. Back then it seemed that you were running away from something. I wish I had known then what I now know about your past, because that insight would have given me a window into your behaviour and it might have helped me understand your seeming indifference towards me and our relationship. Today, I am aware of the horrific past that led to your insensitivity and believe you are entirely blameless.

I recall Mum's worry and preoccupation with our lack of money. And I remember your many arguments with Mum because of her limited food budget. Some unspoken down-turn had clearly occurred in your life. You seemed to take less interest in the world at large with each day that passed, and your financial situation rapidly deteriorated along with your health. Mum began working in an office to make up the shortfall, and sometimes I heard her arguing with you about your careless largesse, which demonstrated your lack of interest in money, the future and life. You made no obvious effort to change things, preferring instead to drift along in a mist of preoccupation, dull routine, and occasional unprompted outbursts of irritation.

In conversation, you always mistook the topic for the person; if you liked someone you also liked their opinion. Your best friend, Jules, was sympathetic to the Soviet Union and believed they could do no wrong. At the 1956 Melbourne Olympics, tensions were already high between the Hungarian and Soviet water-polo teams because on 4 November 1956, Soviet tanks had rolled into Hungary. The polo match took place on 6 December 1956 against the background of the 1956 Hungarian Revolution. The match became known as 'Blood in the Water' because it culminated in a fight and Hungarian player Ervin Zádor emerged during the last two minutes with blood pouring from above his eye after being punched by Soviet player Valentin Prokopov. If my memory serves me correctly, Jules was sympathetic to the Russian position, and to you, Jules could do no wrong.

When Paul was in London in the sixties and you and Mum were about to visit him, Paul asked if the three of you could go back to Poland to visit your family home. Your response was short and succinct. 'I will never set foot in that country ever again.' It seemed to me, naively, that you believed the Second World War was very simple, at least to the limited extent that you spoke about it in front of me and, indiscriminately, in front of many others. I could have summarised it like this, 'The Poles did the bidding of the Nazis and in many ways were worse.'

In researching our family history I discovered that one night in 1933, Nazi storm troopers broke into your home with their Alsatian dogs barking and guns at the ready and threw you and your family onto the street; in 1936 you came by boat to Australia; in 1938 your father committed suicide; on 1 September 1939 your sister and brother (an accomplished pianist who had won the prestigious Paderewski Piano Competition) left Warsaw to escape the Nazis. They were thought to be going to Vilna and were never heard of again. In 1941 your mother, who was in the Warsaw ghetto, breached curfew and was shot dead in the street. Is it any wonder you had such hatred for the Poles?

On 11 February 1942 you walked between the sombre grey columns of the Melbourne Town Hall into the cavernous tiled room filled with desks and tables to enlist. The Pacific had fallen to the Japanese. That was when you joined up. You served with the 2/3 Field Ambulance

9th Division AIF as a medic and stretcher bearer and were sent to the Middle East. You and your wartime mate, Rudi Jaeger, followed on the heels of the medical staff and 'leapfrogged' from one forward position to another at the second battle of El Alamein to carry the wounded from the battlefield. The heat from the desert rose up like a wall.

Nothing could have prepared you for New Guinea. You had some jungle training, on the Atherton Tableland, but I suspect it was like taking swimming lessons in a sandpit. When you landed at Milne Bay in early August 1943 and walked into the clearing station, there were wounded and dying everywhere. Some nights you had to sleep in the rain, sitting against a tree or lying on a log on the ground. Rudi told me, 'The jungle is a very spooky place in wartime. A lot of men came out with bad nerves. Probably your dad did also.' Your division landed at Scarlett Beach in the dead of night. Torpedo boats were approaching in a blaze of bullets; planes were thundering overhead, lighting the surface of the sea, setting fires and destroying villages. Not long after Scarlett Beach you went back to Borneo and returned home in April 1946.

When I was called up to fight in Vietnam it must have been your worst nightmare. No doubt you wanted to protect me from the horror of war, but I suspect your immediate distress was that it reminded you of your own horrendous experiences and loss during the Second World War. I recall, amongst a handful of bills and local circulars, the protruding edge of a long white envelope that turned my stomach like sour milk. In the right-hand corner was the black insignia of the Department of Labour and National Services. I took the mail into the house and handed you and Mum your letters, then took mine to my room and stared at it for a long time, as though it might vanish with the same suddenness with which it had appeared. I didn't need to open it. The black, featureless type of my name spelled out a long, dreaded, intolerable sentence.

Between the letters, I could breathe the bitter smoke of the Vietnamese sky, full of the smell of blood and cordite; the blades of the helicopters rolling over the villages; the crater-scarred fields; children running; bodies scattered along creeks and rivers.

Back then I tried to find a part of my being that was not revolted by the senseless chaos. I thought about my friends, the intense, passionate, anti-war protesters and their rock-hard certainty that the war was wrong and unjust.

That evening, at dinner, I stared at my food with a washed-out feeling of unreality. I looked at you quietly chewing the meat Mum always cut up into small pieces for you since your illness.

I remember the photograph of you in your army uniform that sat on the mantel. You know about these things, I thought. For once, you can help me. I steeled myself to ask you a direct question.

'Dad,' I said, my voice sounding hollow in the quietness of the room, 'Can I ask you something?'

The silence was thicker than before. I started again awkwardly.

'I got a letter from National Service. My number came up.'

Slowly, you put down your fork. You stared at me for a long time, with an indescribable look on your face.

'You were in the war. I thought you could help me.'

You looked down, picked up your fork and continued to eat in silence. I tried again.

'I know it was difficult in those days – but there was a good reason to fight,' I ventured. 'And I would have done the same thing.'

'You don't know what you're talking about,' you said in a low voice, without looking up.

'It's not the same thing in Vietnam. It's wrong.'

You looked up. 'All war is wrong,' you said quietly, and began eating again.

'But Dad,' I said, 'you told me yourself that this war in Vietnam is a mistake. This time we're the ones who are doing the killing.'

You looked as though you wanted to say something but didn't know how to begin.

'I feel like we're doing the same thing. When people supported Hitler …'

Abruptly you stood up. 'That's it,' you shouted, banging your fist on the table. 'Don't talk about things you know nothing about.' All the blood had rushed to your face. You raised your hand to bang on the table again, then stopped in mid-gesture and just stood there, veins bulging in your temples. After a few moments your colour returned to normal, and your arm fell to your side. You met Mum's gaze, and she looked down at the table then began clearing the dishes. You mastered yourself with an effort, mumbling a little, and sat down again.

You will recall I was studying when I was called up and was able to postpone my medical examination until I finished my final exams. A few years later, when I had completed my studies, I joined an underground peace organisation called the Congress for International Co-operation and Disarmament (CICD). The army took the view that service in the jungle of Vietnam would be likely to aggravate skin irritations such as dermatitis, making those soldiers who suffered from it a liability.

Before attending my army medical, I visited a Melbourne doctor who had been recommended by the CICD. He explained to me how to irritate my skin so that I might fail my medical. On his advice, the night before my army medical examination, I rubbed cream on various joints and other parts of my body and wrapped them up in bandages so that the skin could not breathe. Sure enough, the next morning my skin was inflamed. Late that afternoon, I went to a building which, if my memory serves me correctly, was in Elizabeth Street, in Melbourne, for the medical examination. Along with hundreds of other men I stripped down to my jocks and stood in line. The place was a crowded hive of activity and the air was filled with nervous energy.

I was confident that I would fail the exam and so I was not particularly nervous. Eventually it was my turn. The examiner saw my red blistered skin and asked me about it. I explained that I had a history of dermatitis and described the symptoms to him. This was, in fact, true, although I did take some poetic licence and embellish my description. He had a concerned expression on his face which pleased me. Everything had gone according to plan and I failed the medical.

Soon after that, in December 1972, the Labor Party, led by Gough Whitlam, won the federal election with its now famous 'It's Time' campaign. The Whitlam government immediately abolished conscription and withdrew Australian troops from Vietnam.

Much later, I asked you again about your war. I was twenty-three years old at the time. It was a Saturday afternoon and the rain was torrential. You were sitting at the dining-room table with a pen in one hand and the form guide in the other. When I asked you the question, I had no idea of the fear and heartache it would cause you. You shuffled uneasily in your seat, a troubled expression on your face, and I could see you did not know how to respond. But I immediately understood that I must never ask that question again. Back then my question was that of a naïve son who was curious about the war, interested in the world he was born into and hungry to understand more about his silent father and his father's family.

I will never know, but had you sought

professional help to deal with your trauma, perhaps you might have been a happier person and had a greater capacity to demonstrate love and affection. You never once spoke of your suffering. I did not discover your trauma until I researched *My Father, My Father*. Everyone you loved was murdered. That, no doubt, scarred you for life.

Thinking back, your contempt for religion seemed a mark of what you had endured. I recall one Passover night at the home of Nellie Goldberg, my mother's cousin. Her husband, Urisz, was a religious man who attended the synagogue regularly and observed all the ritual of the high holy days. I watched him carefully all evening. After the meal, I asked Nellie what he was saying, but she shushed me with, 'He's just davening.' She continued,

'It's the story of the Exodus from Egypt.'

Urisz stopped and turned to me.

'You should have learned these things already,' he said.

Then he turned back to his praying, the deep, throaty consonants and chanting vowels of his Hebrew. Then the rhythm of the prayer faltered. Another loud recitation was coming from the other side of the room. It took a moment to recognise that it was my father's voice. He was sitting at the table. In a loud voice, he was reciting the winners of the daily double and the trifecta from Saturday's Sporting Globe.

My father read on and on while Urisz stood in the middle of the floor with an indescribable look on his face. After a while, my father finished reading the page and folded up the paper. He got up to go. As he walked past, Urisz said to him, 'You bring shame on this house.' He spat out the words like a curse. My father stopped and looked at him.

'It's all rubbish,' he said. 'We are living in Australia now.'

'You are a Jew,' Urisz said, then pointed to me. 'Your son is a Jew. And he knows nothing of his people.'

My father shrugged contemptuously.

'What is there to know?' he said. 'All this muttering and ranting. It didn't help.' He shook his head. 'There is no God. If there was, he wouldn't have let six million Jews die.'

I appreciate your desperation to forget your fraught past and I suspect tattooing the word Australia on your arm when you first arrived in your new country was a failed attempt to forget your past and start life afresh.

In January 1979, you underwent a triple bypass operation. It saved your life, but only at a price: during the operation you suffered a further heart attack and stroke, which left you partly paralysed, unable to work again. You were fifty-nine. After the operation you became depressed and quiet and seemed to lose the will to live. You were very different to the man dressed as a jockey at Sol and Mita Simons' tenth wedding anniversary. Sol had been dressed as Samson, with a tunic and a huge black mane of flowing locks, and Mita was Delilah, sporting an impressive cleavage and wielding a large pair of scissors. At midnight, the lights suddenly went out, and there was dead silence for a few moments. Then the lights flashed on and a man dressed as a jockey entered the room mounted on a horse. A loud speaker blared, 'And its Cheeky Chap, edging ahead on the last bend, yes Cheeky Chap into the straight, followed by Martaz, and Florilles, and it's Cheeky Chap, Cheeky Chap for the win.' The party broke into applause, and you, in a jockey's peaked cap and jodhpurs, climbed down from your precarious perch on top of your two friends who were suffering badly from heat stress inside the horse costume. You walked over to Mum, who was dressed in the style of the roaring twenties, and proceeded to get roaring drunk.

After your surgery you retreated into your illness. It was an excuse, a relief. You refused to go out and the only people you wanted to be with were your cousin Mary and Frank Klepner. I am surprised to realise how angry I was with you for giving up, for sitting day after day in the same dining-room chair, for all the illnesses and the strokes and the hospital rooms, for walking with a limp, dragging your leg along like a dead weight.

You died doing what you loved. It was a Friday night and you were at your regular poker game. I was told by one of the players that your eyes suddenly widened, you fell forward and collapsed onto the table. You were taken to Prince Henry's Hospital and by the time Mum, Paul and I arrived you were unconscious.

The next morning Paul and I walked into the quiet ward and over to the bed in the corner. After a few moments Paul left to find the doctor. Standing in the room alone I became aware of the strangeness between us. I watched your chest rising and falling with your weak, shaky breaths and I found myself concentrating very hard to recognise this pale shell as you.

It seemed to me that, for a time, standing there in the hospital room, somehow you had been stolen from me. And here, lying before me, was the warm, breathing body of the thief who had stolen you. In your place, the thief had left a stranger: blank, distant, unreachable. I felt a faint, dull stirring, for the first time in many years. For a moment I was a child again, and I felt angry that you had disappeared.

The nurse came in and saw me standing there next to the bed.

'It's all right,' she said, 'you can hold his hand if you like.' I looked at her, and I could see that it was expected of me. I was supposed to be the son. I waited until she had gone, then prepared myself for this strange act. As I reached out, I fought against a feeling of stark discomfort. At last, after a long hesitation, my fingers touched your hand. Your skin was white and papery, with only the faintest hint of clammy warmth, the life that held on somewhere in the weakened organism. The last time I could remember your touch before that was as a little child, having ointment rubbed on my skin for some routine childhood malady.

Between my hand and yours, there was more than forty years of distance and failed affection. I wondered for a moment if, as you lay there beached and helpless on the white bed, the time and the distance might vanish like a single breath. But it was too far and too late. I sat down, holding your hand.

I looked around the room to see if anyone was watching. I felt awkward and embarrassed sitting in the chair with your hand, this stranger's hand, in mine. I moved restlessly in the chair. I could not rid myself of the sense that I was not myself but someone else, standing in a far corner of the room, watching this farcical scene unfolding. I listened to your breaths, rasping slightly in the quiet of the room. That morning I felt pity, sitting there watching your life fading away. But it was the pity of a stranger. When I felt that enough time had passed, I took my hand from yours, and laid your arm carefully back on the white sheet. Then I sat for a long time and stared at the patterns on the floor.

When Paul returned with the doctor, he explained that you had suffered a cerebral haemorrhage and if you were to survive you would have no cognitive function. We agreed that you be made comfortable and given morphine to ease your passing.

You were sixty-five at the time and your death brought to an end twenty years of illness, which, I suspect, resulted in part from many more years of mental torment before that. Standing at your graveside I felt an overwhelming sense of relief. The thick silence that had reigned between us would now pass at last into the permanent stillness of soil and stone – nothing could be changed any more, no one would hope or be disappointed. I could now put our troubled relationship behind me and start life afresh, and yet I was troubled by a sense of unreality. The wooden casket was much too light to hold the weight of a life. I wondered briefly if you had simply evaporated into the air. I looked carefully at the faces of the people around me. Many of them were trembling and tear-stained. I wondered what had touched their hearts so strangely. What could you possibly have given them that could be repaid with such an outpouring of emotion? When it came to my account, the ledgers were empty. I felt nothing, as though I was looking down into a hollow grave. If I wished for tears, it was only to wash away the feeling of dryness that the Melbourne rain could not assuage.

During your illnesses, hospitals had become places of desperation and despair. I had grown to hate them. And after your demise I took detours to avoid any hospital. It wasn't until my first child, Amy, was born that I realised that they can be a force for good – a place that gives life, rather than takes it.

You never spoke to me about yourself, your feelings and your past. Your silence inhibited our relationship. If I was to sum up my perceptions of you, I would say silent, emotionally aloof and remote. And what's more, I reproached you for it as if it were your fault, as if you might have been able, with a mere flick of a switch, to arrange everything differently. Many years later I came to realise you were not in the slightest bit at fault.

You never realised your full potential. I recall one evening at Mary and Frank Klepner's talking about you and the family. We'd reached the end of the conversation and when I left the house, Frank walked me to the car.

'There's one thing I can say,' Frank said. 'Your dad was an intelligent man, a really smart man, and he had a lot of potential. Everyone could see it. But there were reasons why it never came to anything in the end. Latching on to Sol Simons was one. He was too easily swayed. The gambling was another. He always kept it under control, but I could see it meant a hell of a lot to him.'

'But why?' I asked.

'I can't say entirely,' Frank said. 'There were lots of reasons. Most of all, I think he missed his dad. I always thought he was trying in his own way to be like him.'

In any case, in many ways we were different and had anyone wanted to figure out in advance how I, the shy, introverted child, and you, the short-tempered father, would be toward one another they could have presumed that you would simply trample me into the ground until nothing remained of me. Now, that did not happen, but perhaps something more terrible happened – we became estranged. The effect you had on me was the effect you had to have.

If I had grown up entirely free from your influence, I would not be the man I am today. With other people you were quite different – interested in what they had to say, engaged in their lives, friendly and always willing to help. I would have been happy to have you as a friend. It is only as a father that you were too distant for me and your inability to show me any love and affection left me with a profound anger that in later life caused severe heartache that manifested itself in the form of migraines.

Further, I have inherited your generosity of spirit, sympathy for the underdog and desire to improve the world we live in. Like you, I have small-l liberal values. I believe it is important to live an ethical life within society; women should be treated equally and have the same opportunities as men; minority groups should have a strong voice and our Indigenous people should be treated with respect.

When I interviewed Sol, we sat in his lounge, sun streaming through the window, drinking coffee and talking. He told me that when you both had the SP bookmaking business you had a system of lay-offs, so if you couldn't cover the bet, you'd lay off part of the stake with other bookies.

I recall he said, 'That meant you had to be bloody quick on your feet to do the sums before the race started.' He smiled. 'That's where your dad came in – Stan had the quickest head for figures I ever saw.'

I started my accounting business in September 1981 and as the business grew, I became more confident and self-assured. Today I am calm, considered and thoughtful in my demeanour. Unlike you, I dislike taking risks. I am focused, determined and have a great desire to achieve.

Of course, I have become who I am as a result of your influence. But not solely as a result of your influence. A close confidant and client of mine, the late Ron Castan AM, QC, once said how lucky we professionals are because, amongst other things, we have the opportunity to meet and befriend people who, had it not been for our profession, would never have crossed our paths. Indeed, Ron and the late Alan Goldberg AO, QC have been great role models for me. I have modelled much of my behaviour on their considered, thoughtful and insightful actions and advice. Their philanthropy set me on a path of charity that has been very gratifying and earned me an Order of Australia. I have no doubt you would have taken great pride in me.

I recall on one occasion Paul coming into my office and looking around at the files stacked neatly on the sideboard, pens in containers on my desk and books parked in alphabetical order on shelves. He said, 'Wow, you're just like Dad.'

'What do you mean?'

'This need for order – it reminds me of Dad.'

'How so?'

'Did you ever see the books Dad kept for his gambling? Immaculate. You would have been proud of him. I looked at them once, when I came back from overseas – and realised I couldn't stand it. He was absolutely anal about keeping records. Filed and recorded everything. He had every single amount written down, for years and years – what he'd bet, what he'd won, the odds, everything. Who knows why? Bizarre. Standing here looking at your office reminds me of him.'

Mum often said she was embarrassed at dinner parties when you would boast about your clever son, the accountant. And I could see how delighted you were when you came into my office and saw me sitting at my desk, hard at work. I recall visiting you one Sunday afternoon.

You were out in the back yard, reading the Racing Guide, while I helped Mum wash up. She asked me how the business was progressing. I told her things were fine. 'Well,' she said, 'Your father always said you were a clever fellow.'

I stopped and watched her scrubbing each dish with methodical care. At first, I didn't believe her. I had never heard you say anything that remotely resembled a compliment or a favourable remark. Still, I couldn't prevent an unfamiliar, warm feeling of pride from stealing over me. To cover this feeling I said, 'Really? I didn't think he cared.'

'No, no,' Mum said, 'he just doesn't show it.'

I know now you were proud of me.

Your inability to show me any love and affection taught me an important lesson. Today, I willingly and openly tell my children and grandchildren that I love them, how proud I am of them and ensure that I am there for them, emotionally.

I have always thrown myself compulsively into their lives, being careful not to invade their privacy and to give them space to grow. When they were younger I was there shouting hoarsely as Amy's basketball team leaped to victory. I spurred Rachel on as she sprinted around the race track. On parent–teacher night I made sure that I saw every single teacher and threw them a few googlies to check they were doing their jobs properly. I was glad to hear that the kids were doing well, and I basked in their achievements. They were happy and confident, the teachers said. All in all, I was very satisfied with the school – it may have been expensive, but I was determined that my children should have everything I never had myself.

I'm lucky that I knew how to be a good father. I've come to understand how much I loved you and how important it is to nurture, guide and tell my children that I love them.

My kids bear that out. Today, they are capable, responsible women. Amy, a qualified dietician and social worker, is married to Deb and they have two wonderful children. And Rachel is a successful exercise physiologist who is married to Joel.

I have tried always to be present and caring and open with my children … I have tried to be a different father from you.

Acknowledgements

I was fortunate to have the assistance of many people while writing this letter. I am grateful for the help of Nan McNab. Her extensive work in editing this letter has been instrumental in making it markedly better. I have greatly benefited from her insights, counsel and assistance. She has been remarkably patient with me, nothing was too difficult, and she was a pleasure to work with.

My heartfelt thanks to Bob Sessions for his support and guidance. His astute and constructive criticisms have been most valuable. He has been a source of great insight and I owe him a huge debt of gratitude for his incredibly generous support. I am truly grateful to him. He gave willingly of his time and I have benefited from his understanding, acumen and direction.

I have also benefited from the endless hours of typing and re-typing by Noni Carr-Howard and Brooke McInnes.

Finally, many friends have been there for me along this journey. They are too numerous to name – you know who you are. Thank you for your support and encouragement. And last but not least, thank you to my family for your enthusiastic support and for helping me keep everything in perspective.

Bernard Marin AM was born in 1950 and graduated from the Prahran College of Advanced Education in Melbourne in 1970. He established his accounting practice in 1981 and currently works with the staff and partners of the practice as a consultant. Bernard has held a number of positions on various boards, including: Treasurer – Melbourne Writers Festival (2005–16), Koorie Heritage Trust (2000–08), and Liberty Victoria (de facto, 1984–92); board member – Australian Centre for Jewish Civilisation (2009–15), Reichstein Foundation (2011–12), Melbourne Community Foundation (2009–10), and Koorie Heritage Trust (2000–12).

Bernard is the author of *Selection in Human Resource Accounting* (1982); a memoir, *My Father, My Father* (Scribe, 2002); *Good as Gold: A Novel* (Harvard Publications, 2017); *Stories of Remembering and Forgetting* (Harvard Publications, 2019) and *Stories of Profit and Loss* (Harvard Publications, 2019). Bernard lives in Melbourne with his wife, Wendy.

www.ingramcontent.com/pod-product-compliance
Lightning Source LLC
Chambersburg PA
CBHW020329010526
44107CB00054B/2034